7 Essentials to Gain Influence for Success in Life, Ministry, and Business

---

Charlana Kelly

7 Essentials to Gain Influence for Success
in Life, Ministry, and Business

Copyright © 2021 by Charlana Kelly

ALL RIGHTS RESERVED.

No portion of this book may be reproduced in any form without permission from the publisher, except as permitted by U.S. copyright law. For permissions, contact: order@speaktruthmedia.com.

Scripture quotations marked TPT are from The Passion Translation®. Copyright © 2017, 2018 by Passion & Fire Ministries, Inc. Used by permission. All rights reserved. ThePassionTranslation.com. Scripture quotations are taken from the Holy Bible, New Living Translation, Copyright © 1996, 2004, 2015 by Tyndale House Foundation. Used by permission of Tyndale House Publishers, Inc., Carol Stream, Illinois 60188. All rights reserved.

Cover design by: SpeakTruth Media Group LLC
Published by: SpeakTruth Media Group LLC www.speaktruthmedia.com

For information about special discounts available for bulk purchases, sales promotions, fundraising, and educational needs, contact by email: SpeakTruth Media Group LLC at order@speaktruthmedia.com.

ISBN 978-1-7364520-7-3 (pb)

Printed in USA First Edition

DEDICATION

This book is dedicated to the passionate ones, those who desire above all things to bring heaven's influence into the earth and see multitudes won to Christ as a result! Whether in life, ministry, or business, they are single-focused and determined to fulfill the mission they've been given.

God knows you by name. He sees your heart, takes note of your ways. He created you for glory, to bring Himself glory, and entrusted you with His heart and His plans for humanity.

May you be strengthened with all might in your spirit, growing to the full stature of that perfect man in Christ. You are a frontline warrior, and God's favor and influence rest upon you.

I'm honored to stand alongside you, champion you, cheer you on, and celebrate your victories. We are in this together; now, let's gain influence to bring heaven to earth so that humanity can know Christ as Savior and Lord as you succeed in life, ministry, and business.

CONTENTS

Foreword 9

Introduction: My Thoughts on Influence................. 17

Essential 1: Pray 25

Essential 2: Listen 37

Essential 3: Honor 47

Essential 4: Invest 57

Essential 5: Authentic 67

Essential 6: Connect 79

Essential 7: Love 87

Final Thoughts 99

Thank Yous & Acknowledgements 103

About the Author 108

Connecting with Charlana....................................109

Foreword

By Pat Blackwell PhD
Writer Counselor Teacher

I met Charlana Kelly 30 years ago, and our paths have intertwined for decades. We are better than friends – we are Spirit sisters! She and husband Chuck were special to my husband and me because they were one of those couples where both of us really liked both. (Believe me, it isn't always like that with couples!) Through the years, we've had many shared moments that bound us together. We served in church together for more than a decade, and while there were times when we didn't necessarily spend a lot of time together, when we did, it was as though we never missed a beat.

Charlana and Chuck attended our daughters' weddings, delivered us to our surprise 25th Wedding Anniversary party, allowed one of our fledgling daughters to live with them for a while, celebrated the births of our grandchildren, worked alongside three of our girls on church staff, and always welcomed us into their home. And then, when tragedy struck, Charlana wrote the eulogy for our daughter and granddaughter's funeral. There are no words to describe the depth of gratitude our family holds for Charlana and Chuck. They have poured into our lives for many years. If our interactions seem one-sided, it is because they are. The Kelly's love us unconditionally and without reservation and expect nothing in return. We love and respect them more than I can adequately express.

I remember ministry times when prophetic words were spoken over Charlana and me, although I remember more about what was declared over her than over me. Once someone said that Charlana would reach nations for Jesus, I remember chuckling under my breath. (I think she chuckled as well.) Now years later, we both marvel at the incredible opportunities God has provided for her to preach and teach throughout the world.

Charlana is the author of more than a dozen books and hosts a syndicated weekly radio program that over 100,000 listeners hear. She is the founder of a successful media company that includes publishing and media production. Her television programming is broadcast weekly to nearly one billion people worldwide. Her educational program, Tools for Triumphant Living, has led hundreds of thousands to Jesus and is still being used for discipleship training throughout the world and in prison/jail ministries as well. Those prophecies have come to pass again and again and again. And frankly, Charlana is just getting started. Great things are still in the works! Talk about God enlarging her tent and expanding her borders! Jabez has nothing on Charlana Kelly!

As you read this book, here are some things you need to know about Charlana. She is the person you always want to engage with because she makes you feel good about who you are! She imbues that your God-given potential is enough. Simply enough! You are enough! What peace and encouragement and motivation and confidence comes from that sincere statement! Charlana will be your mentor, coach, and cheerleader to see that you accomplish your goals and do so with contagious joy and love that casts out any fear of failure, criticism, or not being enough.

The principles in this book — to pray and listen and connect and be authentic, for starters — are biblical principles revealed for the purpose of influencing people to come to Jesus, the essentials of influence. Our ultimate influence as salesmen, educators, media producers, community builders, or world changers is to bring people to Jesus.

When I received the revelation of that through Charlana's teaching and mentorship, my perception of the world changed, and so much for the better. Suddenly (and it was suddenly, albeit a long time coming!) that revelation opened my eyes and heart in such an exciting way. I realized that every situation — conflict, delay, celebrations, discussion, interaction — had but one end goal: to influence others for Jesus! So, my outlook changed, as did my behavior! My patience grew longer, my tone became softer, my words kinder, and my willingness, even longing, to do kingdom business for Jesus became my driving force! And THAT, my friends, is INFLUENCE! What greater purpose can our influence have than to change for good the heart of another?

Now I'm not an entrepreneur nor a marketplace minister nor a politician making policy, nor anything that one might consider a person of influence. But my role as mother, daughter, spouse, neighbor, consumer, and yes, churchgoer defines my arena of influence. And the goal of my influence is to influence others for Jesus! Charlana taught me that, and this book is the culmination of those lessons.

The 7 Essentials to Gain Influence for Success in Life, Ministry and Business is no ordinary book. I have described the impact of influence in my personal life in part but know well that these same dynamic essentials apply in every arena you enter every day. These are God-inspired, scripture-based notions that have been proven true again and again. Some might say, "well, these aren't really about influence, but about love." Perhaps they are right. When we walk in and consistently practice these steps, the result IS love, and the impact of love on the world has no bounds! These tried and tested methods have helped Charlana Kelly grow into the successful woman she is, and she is about to mentor you to success as well.

So find a comfy chair and a highlighter and get ready! You are about to change! Your life is about to change! And your ministry! And your business! And you are being guided by a kind and gentle, wise, and wonderful, Spirit-led woman of God. Buckle up, my friends. It's going to be an amazing ride!!

By Pastor Leon Wallace

Once again Charlana Kelly has written a life-changing book. I have known Charlana now for five years. During that time, she has challenged and inspired me with her life and writings, and this book is no different.

Charlana has a passion for Christ that few have and she demonstrates a balance in ministry that gives great weight to her words. She is simply exceptional and a great leader of women and minister of the Gospel.

Leadership has been one of my favorite subjects over the past 40 years of ministry. I have read many books on the subject, attended multiple conferences, and taught on this subject frequently. That is why I am so excited about what Charlana has written.

7 Essentials to Gain Influence for Success in Life, Ministry, and Business is filled with insights and principles from praying, listening, loving, etc., that will help a person navigate life in a more efficient way. Charlana highlights leadership characteristics in a way that is simple yet profound, and she leaves a roadmap that anyone can follow to become a better leader.

If you are looking for a guide to greater leadership and a challenge to become a more well-rounded person this book is for you.

Senior Pastor of GSF Church in Crockett TX

President of Standing with Crockett

a Community Nonprofit

INTRODUCTION

My thoughts on gaining influence—the need for it and the fruit of it.

Now, more than ever, we need to influence the world around us. With division and strife at an all-time high among people, believers need to be able to bring an answer with the wisdom of God to every situation, whether in our families, churches, communities, or the cultural arenas of our day.

What do I mean by cultural arenas? These are places of influence where God calls you to impact people with the Gospel. When we think of an arena, we often think of sports, but an arena is also a place of activity, debate, and conflict[1]. These are the places that shape future generations' thoughts and ideas, including our children, grandchildren, and beyond. Areas we must engage in if we are going to ensure our foundation of Judeo-Christian values remain strong for them. These places of influence include family, church, education, business, arts and entertainment, media, and government.

If we want to make a difference, we will have to get into the arena, which might be a terrifying thought. It means that you will have to speak and do what God inspires you to do. You probably don't feel like you are ready for either, but nevertheless, those Holy Spirit nudges keep the pressure on from what sometimes feels like every direction. Here's the good news, what God calls you to do, He graces or empowers you for the fulfillment of it.

From the moment you said "yes" to the Lord, you have been growing in grace and influence, which is precisely what you need to do before you will be effective in those cultural arenas. Even Jesus grew in grace and strength during His early years (Luke 2:52). Remember, He was a man and subject to all things human. As He grew, we must grow in character, stature, and strength as we are prepared to represent God while advancing the Gospel effectively.

Which cultural arenas has God inspired you to influence? We are all called to impact our family and church. I personally have three areas outside of family and church, where God has given me favor and influence; business, media, and government. These are places where I have open doors, relationships, and success every time I have the opportunity to share something that will influence a decision or person in those areas.

We gain influence in life, ministry, and business as we learn how to maneuver these arenas. In order to be effective, our growth is meant to fulfill God's plan of redemption, reconciliation, and restoration of broken people and places to God (Isaiah 61:4).

Influence from a biblical perspective means simply to flow; IN-fluence in, into, or on. A spiritual power (Divine influence) or subtle, invisible power to persuade or dissuade minds and hearts, through words and ideas, that when released are moving, compelling, and inducing[2].

Influence happens as we live our life for Jesus. It's a byproduct of the Holy Spirit working in and through us. Sometimes we get in sticky situations when we try to influence a person or people outside of God's timing using less than desirable tactics. Let me explain what I mean. We see this magnified in the government arena today. There's so much conflict there but no voice of reason. Not many persuasive voices prevail because everyone is defensive. We will never be effective as long as we are the argument rather than the answer. We must learn to look for ways to give a correct word in season with the wisdom of God. His ways are the only ways that will prevail in the end, nothing more, nothing less. So, believers must be able to articulate the ways of God with integrity and honor at the right time so that those who hear can see.

Our influential effectiveness begins with personal pursuits of growth in the character of our lives. In Proverbs 3:3 & 4, Solomon revealed that we gain favor with God and man when we are devoted and faithful to Him. People who are faithfully devoted to God allow Him to form and shape the quality of their character so that they will be able to stand through whatever adversity may come when they enter these areas.

The 7 Essentials you are about to learn are the outworking of our devotion and the benchmarks of the character we need to possess if we are going to be a person of influence. As we grow in each, we gain influence and grow in favor. As you discover how to apply these essentials in your life, you will be successful and find yourself in high places with people who are reconciling and restoring every sphere of influence God has entrusted to their care.

The influence that you have is meant to impact the behaviors, attitudes, opinions, and choices of others. For a Christian, our influence is heaven's influence: God, Jesus, Holy Spirit, the Word, Truth, Wisdom, Knowledge, Understanding, etc. We are created to bring the influence of heaven to earth and impact the world around us.

Influence is NOT power or control; it's not about manipulating others to get your way. As we learn to wield our influence, we will impact the world and people around us; from the least to the greatest in stature.

Now that you understand influence, here are the 7 Essentials that will shape your character and make a difference in every encounter you have with people.

You must learn to operate in your life with these seven essentials as a foundation from which you live. Put each essential into practice, and you will succeed in your life, ministry, and business.

Endnotes

1. Definition | Arena | Merriam-Webster Online Dictionary | https://www.merriam-webster.com/dictionary/arena

2. Definition | Influence | KJV Dictionary Online |

Essential No. 1

PRAY

Essential #1: Pray

One of the most vital parts of a believer's life and integral to a leader's life is prayer. It is absolutely essential to gaining influence.

When I get out of sorts, hurried, worried, stuck, stagnant, whatever, I recenter myself in prayer and focus on God through devotion. More than twenty years ago, I founded the nonprofit Christian Women's Coalition and led a team of women who preached, taught, discipled, and brought healing to women in jails, prisons, transitional homes, and shelters, as well as traveled with me to minister both in and out of the country. Every time we came off a mighty move of God through the ministry we had released, I'd tell them, put that on the altar, give it back to God. He has more extraordinary things, and we don't want to make that moment a monument of worship. Remember it, rejoice, praise God, but let it go so you can be enlarged and empowered to do the next thing.

We can't live on the mountain top; we're not meant to live full time there. We live in the valley with lots of growth, lush beauty, and fresh running water. When we let go, give everything to God, that's when enlargement, promotion, and upgrades come. He always has more for us; we have to position ourselves to receive.

We witnessed magnificent miracles over the years, and we also prayed diligently every single Saturday of the week for many years. Those times of prayer are what birthed the plans and purposes of God corporately and individually. It also brought unity with singleness of heart and mind. Those were glorious times I would not trade for any amount of money or treasure the world could offer.

Your prayer life is the foundation you must build upon in life, ministry, and business. Anywhere you want to influence for Christ, you must pray first. Your prayer life is about that vertical connection with God, and it must not lay dormant or be broken.

Daniel is our great example. He was a devout man of God. He was devoted to prayer and took time during the Hebrew hours of prayer (3 am, 6 am, 9 am, Noon, and 3 pm) to go to the place of prayer. Daniel's faithfulness to pray to God was used against him. King Darius' rivals tricked him into decreeing that no one could pray to anyone other than the king for 30-days. Ultimately Daniel was sentenced to death in the Lion's Den as a result. Even after he learned his fate, he didn't pray for himself. He opened the window toward Jerusalem and prayed for God's people.

Great leaders are selfless, and they want the best for everyone else. They are not clamoring for their own interests or promotion. They look for ways to promote others and desire redemption for all. They pray redeeming prayers. Their prayer influences every place.

No matter what your position in life, prayer is vital. Pray always, in every place. Start with prayer and finish with prayer. Keep your heart before the Lord throughout the day, be easily entreated by Him. Seeking the heart of God and asking from your heart in every matter. I love The Passion Translation, especially Philippians 4:6 & 7 when it comes to prayer;

> "Don't be pulled in different directions or worried about a thing. **Be saturated in prayer throughout each day**, offering your faith-filled requests before God **with overflowing gratitude**. Tell him every detail of your life, then God's wonderful peace that transcends human understanding will guard your heart and mind through Jesus Christ."

Gratitude is essential in prayer. Discipling yourself to stay focused in prayer will increase your effectiveness across the board. Know where you are supposed to be and stay there. Stop looking around at what everyone else is doing and saying.

If you are easily distracted by the opinions of others, you could be entangled with the fear of man. Identify it quickly because being concerned about what others think will halt progress. Stop using the opinions of men to gauge the effectiveness of your actions or response. The thoughts of others do not move leaders from their assigned posts. They are motivated by God alone. Only the inspired words of God will stand the test of time.

They will be upheld throughout history, nothing else. The rest will fall to the ground dead because they did not come from God. Pray and get your instruction from Him.

Prayer paves the road ahead of you and opens the door for God to move. Nothing happens without prayer first. Reese Howells, the great man of prayer, once said, "History belongs to the intercessor." Yes, it does! Because their prayers are Divine, God-breathed, and they produce exactly what God desires to do. Whether proclamation, declaration, supplication, or intercession all come from the Throne of God. Even worship is a form of prayer, in fact, the highest form of prayer.

When you get stuck or hit an obstacle, prayer should be your first response. It will move things out of the way and give you the wisdom you need to move forward. Ask for more wisdom; it is the principal thing, and when we ask, God gives more than enough for the task at hand. Remember this; *prayer paves, wisdom reveals.* Sometimes though, we need to change and realign ourselves with God to move forward. He will hold us in a place until we recognize the need and respond with the right heart.

Sometimes too, people need to go from our lives. Be sensitive to the voice of God and the prompting of the Holy Spirit. He will show you exactly what to do and how to do it when you seek Him in prayer.

The key is to pray, do not forsake prayer. It is necessary for every role of your life. Whatever things you ask in His name, He will hear you, and you will have whatever you ask. You have not because you ask not or ask according to your desires. Tell God everything in prayer. How you feel, what you see, what you want, everything. No small prayers either; ask big audacious prayers. You will be blown away as God starts to answer and fulfill those bold asks.

When I started working in the media industry, I began with podcasting, cohosting with friend Janet Marie Napper on Overcoming Abuse God's Way. Soon after, her producer asked me to host my own program. I agreed and promptly made a list of all the guests I wanted to interview on my podcast. One name on that list was Dr. Martin Luther King Jr.'s niece Dr. Alveda King, a prominent woman in politics, pro-life, and the church. She often guested on networks like Fox and CNN. She also was a Georgia state legislator and had been instrumental in advancing a conservative, pro-family agenda. I wasn't prepared for how quickly God would make that request a reality! But He did, and she guested on my podcast shortly after I wrote that list! I thought, "Who me? Little Charlana Kelly?" God is looking to elevate anyone and everyone who will dare to ask in prayer and be faithful with what He gives them.

God put those dreams in your heart. It wasn't Charlana's big dream; God desired to bring that to pass. If you have a pure heart and desire to bring God glory through your life and work, there is no limit to where He will take you, so pray, ask away, and believe. And, don't be surprised when things happen quickly.

Ask Him to enlarge your capacity to influence through prayer. There will be a price to pay as God gives you more. There will be crushing from time to time. Remember, though, the crushing produces great anointing in your life. Crushing brings us closer to God and into closer alignment with His plans. Only those faithful with least will be made ruler of much. The work is worth it. He only requires us to be faithful with what is in our hands. Walk with Him and leave all other matters to Him. Don't think about the how, when, where, don't waste time on those questions. Spend your time in prayer, seeking God. Just keep praying bigger. Mark 11:24;

> "This is the reason **I urge you to boldly believe** for whatever you ask for in prayer—be convinced that you have received it, and it will be yours."

Also, be mindful of where your feet stand and the pathway you walk upon every day. When we take the ground in prayer, we open doors for God's people to move into that place. Praying people are like doorkeepers advancing the cause of God, not their own.

A mark of a seasoned leader and pray-er is the lack of personal pronouns. Those who lose themselves in Christ will advance and enlarge quicker. They understand this is God's work. They know they are entrusted with the people and places and that they will give an account to God about how they handled both. Matthew 28:19;

> "Now **wherever you go, make disciples** of all nations, baptizing them in the name of the Father, the Son, and the Holy Spirit."

You must take the nations or cities where you are called to influence in prayer first. God has given you that ground to redeem, rebuild, repair, and restore for His glory. When the enemy buffets, we answer, "NO, you may not have this nation, city, or people. It or they belong to the kingdom of God, to Christ Himself. And, I am taking it back, in the name of Jesus!"

We must grow in the field God has given us before He will enlarge it. Be faithful daily, pray over your field and people, ask God how to redeem it for Him? Ask Him to show you what adjustments and changes need to be made in your life so that you can advance into more significant places of influence.

Remember,

- Always pray first about everything (Phil. 4:6 & 7).
- Prayer is the single MOST POWERFUL thing you can do regarding any matter.
- Prayer opens the door for God to move in your life/circumstance.
- Prayer paves the road ahead of you!
- Prayer is the most essential part of leadership, whether in relationships, ministry, or business.
- Ask God to enlarge your territory and increase your influence (1 Chron. 4:10).
- When you ask, it's His good pleasure to say "Yes!"
- So, be BOLD in prayer! ASK! (Mark 11:24)

- You are here to advance the kingdom of God and impact the world around you (Matt. 28:19).
- Your influence will enlarge your field as you take back people and nations for God.

"Don't worry about anything, pray about **everything**..."
(Philippians 4:6a)

List the top 7 things you are asking God for that will help you gain influence.

1. _____
2. _____
3. _____
4. _____
5. _____
6. _____
7. _____

Essential No. 2

LISTEN

Essential #2: Listen

Listening will empower you to influence people in your field, vineyard, and the cultural arenas you are called to impact today. These character qualities must be developed in you before God will trust you with the big things. When you are faithful with the least, God will make you ruler over much! We first prove ourselves in our prayer closet, listening to God. We must get our instructions from Him alone.

Listening is a lost art today. A woman of influence listens more than she speaks because listening is the better part of communication. Proverbs 1:5 says, "A wise man will hear…" When you turn your ear toward the one you want to influence, you can gain understanding and receive the instruction he needs to hear.

Among the more prominent words in the Hebrew meaning of "listen" like hearken, heed, and pay attention, there is an unusual word, "auscultate," which means taking a stethoscope and listening to the heart. Before we can influence anyone, we need to hear their heart. Most people listen at a very superficial level, listening to answer only, even while the other person is talking. So, bottom line, we're not listening at all. Wisdom waits to respond and listens not only with the ear but the heart.

Isn't it interesting the root word "ear" connects hear and heart!!! The ear is the gateway to the heart, and vice versa, but neither will be engaged if we aren't listening. The value of a fully engaged ear and heart cannot be overstated. We gain wisdom and influence when we listen to a matter so we can discern what is necessary for our answer. Not surprising that Solomon, the wisest man of all, requested a "hearing or understanding heart" when God asked him what He could do for him. King Solomon desired such a gift so that he could rightly judge the situations God's people brought before him. Solomon asked for the best gift God could give and received, in addition God's promise of a long life, riches, and honor.

Waiting is required to listen. Wait for the other person to finish talking. Don't be quick to answer either. If you have no idea what to say, tell them you will get back to them with an answer. There are no requirements for an immediate response. Sometimes people just need a listening ear. Not just to dump on but to truly hear them out. Even with aggravated people who want to tell you what has happened, if you let them talk until they can't talk anymore, they are disarmed and ready to hear what you will say to them.

Practice, practice, practice listening. Ask for the correct answer; the wisdom this person needs, influence will result.

Not long ago, I was asked to speak at a City Council meeting regarding an annual event integral to the success of our small historic town. First, I was honored to be asked to speak. Secondly, I didn't want to say what everyone else said, which usually happens. If you pay attention, very seldom do people have something new to add to the discussion. It ends up being a reiteration of old information, or people often say, "I agree with what 'so-and-so' said."

I asked God to give me the answer. Almost everyone reiterated the importance of having the event due to the financial windfall it brought to our local businesses. When it came time for me to speak, I was prepared. I listened, I heard God, and I talked about the need for connectivity during a season when we were coming out of lockdown due to Covid. I also spoke about allowing the people to self-govern; America was established on this idea, believing that the majority of people will choose what's best for everyone when governing their lives. I wasn't a parrot, I had something of wisdom to share, and I'm sure it made a difference in the thoughts of our city councilmen and women.

Everyone has something to say but is what they say bringing impact and change. We're all passionate about what we believe, too; if we are not willing to listen to those we disagree with, we will never have an opportunity to influence their beliefs.

I heard Kenneth Copeland say, "One word from heaven can change your life forever." He's right! Let's endeavor to receive the "one word" and release it. Wisdom plus one word will have a powerful ripple effect and touch more lives than you can imagine.

Another way we can influence people by listening and giving the correct answer is to ask questions. We don't need to give a statement back to them and tell them everything they NEED to know or do. Just ask a few pointed questions that lead them to conclude the correct answer. Like;

> Have you thought of it this way?

> Have you considered this?

As you ask questions, you are giving them an opportunity to see from a different perspective.

Unfortunately, the majority of people don't think critically anymore. They don't make deductions based on facts. Often never seeking out the rest of the story. Reading headlines and tweets thinking the whole truth can be found there. We must dig deep to discover the facts and hear all sides.

As you listen, don't forget, love is the license to speak. Resist the natural urge to rush in with your thoughts, build relationships by interacting with them more and more. You may not influence them the first time you listen to their thoughts, leave the door open for more conversation, and you will gain their trust, and they will open their hearts and minds to receive.

Do not the thoughts of others, only the influence of Jesus, the Word, the Holy Spirit. You listen to people so that you can influence them, not the other way around. Don't compromise your beliefs or morals; hold firm to your convictions. God wants to use you to bring His influence into the earth, not so much in the church where we are already like-minded, but outside the church where people need the TRUTH, Jesus.

Make listening your daily habit, and you will see the fruit of heaven in your life and the lives of others.

Remember,

- Listening is a lost art form today.
- Listening is the better part of communication.
- Practice listening.
- Resist the human response that wants to answer before hearing the words and heart of the person talking.
- Exercise restraint, stay calm and collected.

- Keep your heart tender towards the person you are listening to so you can hear.

- As you listen, ask God to give you the answers and wisdom people need.

- While listening, the Holy Spirit will reveal every detail, and you will be positioned to release His Words with the kind of power that will change hearts and minds.

- Make listening a daily habit, and you will see the fruit of heaven in your life and every person you encounter.

"Make your ear attentive to wisdom, incline your heart to understanding" (Proverbs 2:2).

List 7 people you will start listening to so that you can allow the Holy Spirit to release the answers and wisdom these people needed.

1. _____

2. _____

3. _____

4. _____

5. _____

6. _____

7. _____

Endnotes

1. Hebrew Definition | Listen | Google Translate | https://translate.google.com/?sl=auto&tl=iw&text=listen&op=translate&hl=en

Essential No. 3

HONOR

Essential #3: Honor

Honor is the basis of all human relationships. We're not going to study The Ten Commandments in this book; however, it bears importance to mention that the four preceding commandments to "honor your mother and father" center around your vertical relationship with God. The five following the command to "honor" focus on your horizontal relationship with others. I also want to establish the fact that the root word for "honor" is "weighty." Honor is a weighty matter, and when we honor, we are releasing the weightiness of God-- His glory!

So, honor is a key to gaining influence. And when you honor others, even those you disagree with, you align yourself with God; His will, His way, His purpose. Peter penned these words that are also a basis for the Christian's life;

> "Honor all men. Love the brotherhood (Christians). Fear God (Reverence and obedience). Honor the king." 1 Peter 2:17

Honor is not a suggested way of life; it is a required character trait for the people of God. We owe honor to ALL people. Even when we disagree and when we are asked to violate God's Word. We still honor. Here's where the rubber meets the road. When we are asked to disobey God, we must respectfully decline while still honoring the authority who commanded us to do so. The most remarkable biblical example of this would be Daniel and his friends, Shadrach, Meshach, and Abednego. They honored the king but refused to obey his ungodly decrees. Like them, to gain influence, which Daniel did in spades, we must learn how to maneuver the courts of unbelieving kings (or people in authority) with honor while strategically advancing the plans of God. When we honor God above all, He takes up our cause and fights for us. We will never lose. If we are currently in a situation that looks like a loss, God is not finished. You must end in faith, in honor, in doing what is right in the sight of God.

George Washington and many leaders who went before and came after him clearly understood the importance of honor. He penned what became the book "Rules of Civility and Decent Behavior in Company and Conversation." Jesuit priests originally wrote the 110 essential rules in France during 1595, then as a school assignment young George Washington penned them again. The President's first rule was regarding respect for others. He noted, "Every act done should show some sign of respect for those that are present."

Respect is a part of honor. The Hebrew words for honor include respect, dignity, homage, credit, esteem, venerate, bestow, revere. Again, all weighty words necessary in our dealings and conversation to gain influence and change people and places.

It is obvious today that we have lost our ability to be civil and to engage people with hopes of influencing them with the truth. As much as we need a revival for salvation. As we interact with others, honor is a character quality that we need to pay attention to in our relationships. Since it is foundational to God's character, it is also to ours. Every word and deed should display honor.

Honor begets honor; as we honor, we will, in turn, be honored. If you honor God, He will honor you. Acknowledge Him before men, and Jesus will acknowledge you before the Father. There's a reciprocal response to everything we do in our lives; the good, the bad, *and* the ugly. As leaders, we must make sure we are not on the "what *seems* right" side of everything but on God's side of everything. When we do this, He will promote us, open doors for us, and give us opportunity. If you are stuck in your life right now, believing for things that have not happened yet, then assess your level of honor.

Do you make everything about you? Or do you look for ways to serve others? Have you dishonored or devalued others? Friend, if you have, you will need to make that right. You will know the answer to those questions by how you react when others are promoted or recognized. Do you get that sick feeling inside, jealous, mad that you're doing the same thing they are, but you never get noticed or celebrated for it? These are signs that you are not honoring people. Also, are you argumentative with people who don't see things the way you do? Are you overbearing, overpowering, and as a result, do you experience division and strife in your life? If so, dishonor is displaying itself in your relationships or interactions.

Every person should leave your life blessed! That bears repeating! Every person should leave your life B-L-E-S-S-E-D! Your heart should desire they outrun, outshine, outachieve everything you do or want to do in life. As you realign yourself with God and people, doors will open.

And, as a leader, when you are in another man's house, honor the authority and the belief structure. For example, when you speak in a Baptist church, know their doctrine, and honor their doctrine. Don't go in and preach/teach against their beliefs. If the pastor asks you to do/not do certain things, then honor his/her request. Support the vision and mission, don't speak against it! If you can't abide by this ethical and biblical protocol, then respectfully decline the opportunity.

Also, regarding culture, honor the culture. If you are traveling out of the country, learn the customs and honor them.

I traveled to India in 2000 on a mission trip. One of the first things we did was attend a team meeting to talk about the dos and don'ts of the culture. It turns out, showing the sole of your shoe or foot was a great insult in Indian culture. Offering your right hand for anything was considered unclean. And the physical cue for saying, "Yes," was not moving your head up and down, but side to side. Each piece of information was invaluable to my time in India as I desired to influence the people with the message of Christ, hoping and praying each one would receive Him as Savior and Lord. If I insulted them, offered unclean things to them, or misread social cues, it could bruise their hearts for Christ.

I can't end this chapter without getting really direct about what's unfolding in the Governmental arena today. There is so much disrespect and dishonor, divisive speech, and anger from believers who frankly have aligned themselves against God. Remember, honor all men, love the brotherhood, fear God, and honor the king? We've had issues with this since the beginning. God's people not understanding the order of God and how all authority comes from Him. Some good, some bad, all serve God's purpose and plan. Even in Paul's day (Acts 23), when the guards struck him in court at the command of Ananias. Paul did not know that he was the high priest of God and spoke harshly to him, accusing him of breaking the law. When he learned of Ananias' position, Paul immediately recanted, quoting the Scripture, *"Do not speak evil about the ruler of God's people."* We can either fight our own battles or let God fight for us. Dishonor puts you in the driver's seat and takes you out from under God's protection. When He said honor all men and love the king, He meant it. And when we live honorably and keep His Word, we are about to influence the hearts and outcomes of ungodly authority. Just like Daniel did and Esther too.

Honoring all men speaks to the love of God who calls them invaluable and worthy of respect. Even our prayers should be honorable, never a "get them, God," always a release of grace and mercy in hopes of that moment of heart-change that opens the door for Christ, which is what our influence is all about. The Gospel.

Remember:

- There cannot be too much made of the power of honor to increase your ability to influence people and places around you.

- Peter wrote, "Honor all people ... honor the king" (1 Peter 2:17).

- The Scripture teaches us we will have a full reward when we value and respect all people.

- We receive a partial reward when we are selective about who we honor.

- There is no reward when we refuse to honor God and people.

- Honor begets honor; when you honor, you will be honored by God and people (Galatians 6:7-9).

- Honor repeatedly opens doors and gives opportunities to people.

"By humility and the fear of the Lord are riches and honor and life" (Prov. 22:4).

List 5 areas where you want God to open a door and give you an opportunity to influence people and advance the kingdom of God. These are the places where you need to look for ways to recognize and honor the people in those places.

1. _____
2. _____
3. _____
4. _____
5. _____

Endnotes:

1. Hebrew Word for Honor | Definition | Etymology | https://hebrew.jerusalemprayerteam.org/glory-honor-respect-dignity/
2. George Washington | Civility | Foundations Magazine | http://www.foundationsmag.com/civility.html

Essential No. 4

INVEST

Essential #4: Invest

It's an unusual word when talking about influence, but trust me, it is an integral part of our ability to impact people and the cultural arenas of our time. To gain influence, we must invest. Think of it along the lines of sowing and reaping; investment = sowing, whether it's your time, talent, or treasure (money).

Invest in the cultural arena you are called to impact. Everyone is called to invest in their family, church, and community. If you own a business, you invest in your business. Your investment determines your success. If you have children still being educated, invest in their education. We all are impacted by entertainment and media. What will you invest in those cultural arenas? Or, will you choose to remove your investment from the things that bring confusion and destruction to you and your family? And, of course, government, we are called to impact our government. Our votes are our voice. Invest in this arena by being fully empowered with the facts and with God's truth. A Christian who votes for ungodly matters is himself ungodly. It reminds me of something Jesus said, where your treasure is, there your heart is also (Matt. 6:21).

Investment involves strategic alignment to bring heaven's influence into the people and places you are called to impact. For me, I have a government and nations call on my life. Whenever I show up in either of those places, power is released, favor is evident, and I am strategically aligned with people moving in those areas.

Back in 2000, I was invited to lead a prayer group with the target of my choice. Because I knew my calling, I said, "I'll pray for government and nations." For ten years, I spent an hour or two weekly praying into these arenas for the plans and purposes of God to be fulfilled.

I had no idea going in that we would be thrust into a season of intense prayer, beginning with the Presidential Election of 2000 when Florida's Presidential Election results would be contested between George W. Bush and Al Gore. God knew! And, He knew what lay ahead on 9/11/2001. And, He knew about the war that would come as a result. When I tell you the wisdom God trusted me and others with during that time was monumental, it's an understatement. I randomly chose Tuesday, not even thinking about elections. Every decision regarding the outcome was released on a Tuesday, *and* often we would pray out phrases and sentences revealed by the Spirit that would then be spoken out of the mouths of officials the next day. It was crazy! I was investing. I invested my time and talent, sowing into governments and nations. The investment was significant and took me to places of favor where I influenced people who made decisions that would potentially shape the future.

Investing is also financial; however, money is low on the totem pole, friends. Yes, give and give generously to the people and places you want to influence. Never put it first, though! Why? It's the most inconsequential part of investing. Even though God will ask you to give, we should never give to receive. Give expecting NOTHING in return, and you will stay right where you need to be in the position of influence you hold.

Investing in the kingdom of God is about the advancement of the Gospel. I liken it also to being a door-opener! Psalm 24 paints the perfect picture, "Lift up your heads oh ye gates (Points of Entry), be lifted up you everlasting doors, for the King of glory to come in…" You and I, we, are entry points for Jesus; gates, and doors that open for Him to move. Just as we are going through these 7 essentials to gain influence, our door opener responsibilities begin in prayer. We will speak too when that door opens, and we know now there is something we are to say.

Paul even asked his fellow believers to pray and ask for a doorway of utterance to be granted to him to speak as he ought to speak and know how to answer each one. Man! That is a prayer we should all be praying daily. God grant me a doorway to speak Your wisdom, release Your plans, and bring salvation to humanity. Let's pray that right now and make it a daily prayer. The wisdom and influence will flow like a mighty river when you do.

We are merely the spokesman, messenger, deliverer, and vehicle God uses to release His wisdom and insight, which is why we must stay in tune with the Holy Spirit and with what God is doing at that moment. We should operate with spiritual insight, awareness, and discernment continuously.

Start paying attention to how you can invest in the people and places you want to influence. Attend meetings, ask questions, speak when you are asked to speak. Be emotionally even, conduct yourself like an ambassador, be light in the darkness. I love Isaiah's words, especially in Chapter 49, when he writes, "Go forth into darkness, show yourselves!" When you show up and release God's answer, hearts and minds will change. Believe me; they want to hear what you have to say when you speak as God's spokesman. Your challenge is to get the heart of God and speak His words, not your opinions.

One way I love to invest in people is to make their hopes and dreams come to pass. Think of that for a moment. All around us every day are people who desire something that we can fulfill for them. There's no greater joy than to watch someone else rejoice that God has provided for them. I learned this a long time ago; all blessing comes through people! Looking for ways to invest in people opens all kinds of opportunities!

Ask God right now to give you a passion for seeing the kingdom of God advance through whosoever will let Him use them. Don't worry. Advancing the call and impact of others will not detract from you. It will enlarge your territory and give you multiplied impact. Trust me; I know this all too well. I've been a witness to it and intend to continue to advance others in everything I do.

Still focus on your field; you're not entering another person's field. Paul even wrote about this in 2 Corinthians 10:15, "We do not boast beyond limit in the labors of others. But our hope is that as your faith increases, our area of influence among you may be greatly enlarged…" His purpose of investing in others was never to take credit for their success but to enlarge his reach with the Gospel. Wisdom from above, friends!

When you set your heart to invest in people, you will increase and multiply everything and everyone around you. There's a shift when you start focusing on how you can add to others. Be that person who brings life and light to all. As you add to others, you too will experience an increase of God's power, presence, favor, and influence in your life, ministry, and business. It's all about relationships. Never look at people thinking what can I get *from* them. Ask, what can I *add* to them?

Nurture relationships by investing. Cheer people on, celebrate their successes, get to know them and their families. Maya Angelou once said, "I've learned that people will forget what you said, people will forget what you did, but people will always remember how you made them feel."

And, I don't mean to throw a monkey wrench in on all this wonderful blessing I'm sharing here, BUT start investing in the people who are the most difficult for you! Oops! Did you just read that? Yes! I can affirm today that every single person who rubbed me the wrong way, as I persevered with them, investing, and loving them, they turned out to be a blessing in my life during a season when I needed what they were about to bring to the table.

You've probably heard that pearls are made from grains of sand rubbing together inside an oyster shell. Yes, friend, sometimes it takes friction to create beauty! Don't let friction cause you to disengage, embrace them and start investing. Show them what it looks like to be a person of influence who walks in the favor of God and man. Trust me; they will notice because they are divinely appointed to your path to help you grow. Never forget that little nugget of truth!

Choose today to be the one who cheers, who celebrates, who encourages, who invests into the people and places God has chosen you to influence! You will be amazed by the eternal fruit produced as you become diligent to invest.

Remember,

- Find ways to invest in the people and places where you want to have influence. Invest in the dreams of others.
- Bring increase to people and everything you touch.
- Bring life!
- Be an adder and a multiplier everywhere, in your family, ministry, and business. People are most important, so invest in relationships.
- Be a cheerleader for others, and you will never lack a cheerleader in your life.

List 7 people or institutions/organizations you can start investing in today. Make a plan for your investment of time, talent, and treasure. Start making contacts with the people or places to implement your plan. Look for ways to serve.

1. _____

2. _____

3. _____

4. _____

5. _____

6. _____

7. _____

Essential No. 5

AUTHENTIC

Essential #5: Authentic

The definition of "authentic" is the adjective or action word of "authenticity," because being authentic requires action on our part.

Authentic always sounds so fun to me. But here's where we can get on the wrong side of being "authentic." We assume it applies to others, how we act towards them, speak to them, etc., which is *NOT* what I am referring to when I talk about gaining influence with people and places. It's about YOU, what you believe about yourself that will shape what you think about others. How you feel about yourself shows up in your self-talk and in the way you treat others. For example, I feel shame, so I shame others, I feel rejected, so I reject others.

If we are to gain influence, we must be our authentic selves, which requires us first to shore up and solidify what we believe about ourselves. So, let's turn the authentic "knife" on our hearts right now to get this essential rooted deeply within us so that we will gain heaven's influence.

Let me start with a personal testimony, I've lost 120 pounds over the last nine years. I've lost it slowly, in 30-pound increments (so happy I did it this way because it became a lifestyle change rather than a quick fix with no growth or advancement). With each level of loss, I learned an important lesson about my emotions and heart condition. The last 30 pounds opened a deep door taking me to an authentic state of being. Let me explain.

During this season, I decided one day to do Dr. Caroline Leaf's 40-day Brain Detox. During the first week, she instructed the participants to sit quietly with the Lord and ask this question, "What do you believe about yourself"? As I sat, eyes closed, heart in tune, listening, I heard, "Self-loathing." I thought, "What?" I do not "loath" myself. Even though I thought I knew what this word meant, I looked it up and was shocked that one of the meanings is self-hatred[1].

I couldn't believe it! I don't hate myself. So, I asked, "Father, why did You say that? Do I *really* hate myself?" He replied with the two greatest commands, "You must love the Lord your God with all your heart, mind, soul, and strength. And, love your neighbor *as yourself.*" He went on and said, "You do everything well, but you skip over loving yourself." I continued to sit with the Lord to reveal the truth of my heart, and sure enough, I found my thoughts (self-talk) lending themselves toward self-loathing. One of the most consistent thoughts I had about myself at that time was, "I am bad." I would think that about myself all the time. It's remarkable the things that will be revealed when we take the time necessary for self-discovery.

As I looked around for examples of what loving myself looked like, I couldn't find an accurate portrayal in today's culture. We have selfie sticks, glamour shots, filters, perfect lives portrayed on social media, and all of it seemed self-centered or selfish in ways to promote whatever is peddled. I thought, "God, I don't know what it *really* looks like to love myself. Tell me." His answer, "You must love what I created you to be, how I created you to look, the gifts I've given you, and what I am doing in your life." Lightbulb moment, okay, now I see.

So, I set my course to intentionally take time to love myself, love what God had created, what God was doing through me, and everything about myself. As a result, an authentic life emerged. And little by little, inferiority, fear, feelings of unworthiness, being unqualified, wanting to hide, shrink back, blend into the crowd all began to dissipate from my heart and mind.

So, the key to being authentic is embracing yourself, falling in love with what God created you to be, celebrating your gifts, your uniqueness, and beauty. Look in the mirror as soon as you can, look at yourself straight in the eyes and say, "I love YOU, I LOVE YOU, I am happy with you." Absolutely, accept and celebrate yourself!

The toxicity of our culture today is twisting and perverting our identity, our gender, and our racial heritage, all intrinsic pieces of loving ourselves. We are teaching children that their inherent identity at birth is wrong; it's a mistake that they were born with particular skin color or created to be a boy or girl. These poisoned perspectives are against God and His creation. They tell Him, He was wrong, perpetuating our feelings of confusion and chaos that set us on a course of self-hatred and destruction.

When God created you (or anyone else for that matter), He created you perfectly, as He saw fit. He created you and said, "She's beautiful, powerful, amazing!" But we often want to be someone or something else. In doing so, we are comparing ourselves to others which ultimately rejects the perfection that God created in us.

Comparison is an identity and purpose killer, along with competing and complaining. When we loath ourselves, that is exactly what we are doing, telling God, "You made a mistake, You were wrong; I reject what You created." God got really clear with me about this matter as He revealed the truth, ultimately saying, "If you reject what I have created, you DO NOT love Me!"

Simply put, and I say this with all the love in my heart, "STOP rejecting yourself and stop rejecting God! "

Since you are reading this book, I know that you are a P-O-W-E-R-F-U-L woman of God. If you are struggling, like I was, you have lacked self-awareness up to now in this same area. Let Holy Spirit test you and see if there are any residues of self-hatred.

Here's a quick test: How do you feel when you are standing in a room full of highly successful, influential people who are movers/shakers? How does your heart feel? Do you feel like you don't belong there? Do you shrink back, become defensive? What do you do when you are demeaned because you are a woman? Do you feel like there's something wrong with you, you're broken, unqualified, unworthy? If you feel like this about yourself, you need to go back to the basics of loving yourself. And, keep doing this until you can stand in that room, know you are chosen to be there, and feel completely empowered and qualified to be there. Not because you have a bunch of letters behind your name, but because God put you there! Operate from the root of loving your uniqueness and power.

Side note here; always honor authority and operate in the order established by that authority, but never compromise who you are and what God created you to be in this life. And, never apologize for your gift. You can't fit any other mold, only His, and as Max Lucado said so eloquently, "When God created you, He broke the mold!" When we operate from that place, we are being authentic, true to what God created.

You might ask, "What if I'm not received?" Then like Jesus told His disciples, shake the dust off your feet and move on.

When you are authentic, it means that you are being a genuine original, real, honest, reliable, dependable, trustworthy, and credible. You see, being authentic is about you, not how you treat others.

When you are genuine, you are not contrived, which means to behave in a disingenuous way. As a woman of God gaining influence, you move ONLY with the Spirit of God. Like Jesus, you are doing and saying only what the Father does and says. Never violate your heart! Honor your heart as the treasure that it is to God. Don't model others; model Jesus. Duplicate Him, and you will act genuinely and be authentic.

Embrace your originality, be real, be honest no matter what. Bathe your honesty in love, mercy, and kindness. People will appreciate your heart. And, if you don't have an answer, stay quiet. You are not required to speak. When you talk out of turn, you are not authentic; you are giving an answer to something God has not asked you to provide.

Reliability is huge in the world of influence and a characteristic of being authentic. Let your word be your bond, your "yes" be yes, and your "no" be no. The most powerful word in the English language is "No!" Billionaire Warren Buffett, the chairman, and CEO of Berkshire Hathaway, has a theory on the power of saying, "No": "The difference between successful people and really successful people," he says, "is that really successful people say no to almost everything[2]." Honor your words, keep your commitments, and be consistent; show up when you say you will! It will prove you are dependable and trustworthy as you gain influence in the arena you are called to impact with the Gospel.

Cultivating credibility is required to be authentic. Always correct your mistakes, hold yourself accountable. This one trait will take you far and bring you before great people of influence. And, you, yourself, will become a woman of significant influence. Jacko Willink, a retired Navy Seal and author of "Extreme Ownership," wrote in his book that great leaders always own the mistakes of his/her team. They never make excuses for anything;

they own it. Friends, that one piece of information will change everything in your life. Don't just own your mistakes; fix them. Your credibility will skyrocket.

Fall in love with what God created you *to be and to do*. You can't get those out of order. Loving your "*being*" must come first. If the doing has come first in your life, ministry, or business, it will never produce the kind of results or fruit you, and God, desire for your life. When your being is shored up and solidified, then your doing will be blessed.

You are a leader, and God wants to increase your influence. You are not called to blend in with a crowd but to stand out, so that the crowd will recognize you and follow you to where God is leading. As you become the authentic you God created, you will be easily recognized, and you will flourish with the people and places you are created to influence!

Remember:

- Trying to be someone else will never give you influence.
- When you get stuck trying to model others, you will ultimately blend in with the crowd. Change

your thinking, believe in the beauty/uniqueness of who you are.

- There's not another YOU.
- Fall in love with what God has created you to be and do.
- Make a mark of uniqueness upon the areas you are called to impact.
- As you do, you will become a leader, not a follower.
- You will stand out from the crowd, and you will have immeasurable joy as God smiles down from heaven seeing you in the fullness of what He created you to be.

Now, list 6 ways to embrace your uniqueness and be more authentic than you ever have been before.

1. _____
2. _____
3. _____
4. _____
5. _____
6. _____

End Notes

1. Definition | Self-loathing | Merriam Webster Online Dictionary | https://www.merriam-webster.com/dictionary/self-loathing
2. Quote | Warren Buffet | "This is Why saying 'No' is the Best Way to Grow Your Career" | Forbes, November 2019 by Amy Blaschka | https://www.forbes.com/sites/amyblaschka/2019/11/26/this-is-why-saying-no-is-the-best-way-to-grow-your-career-and-how-to-do-it/?sh=3772641c479d

Essential No. 6

CONNECT

Essential #6: Connect

One of the essential things for bringing influence to people and places is connection. The Apostle Paul gave the greatest example of what connection looks like in 1 Corinthians 9:19-22

> "Even though I am a free man with no master, I have become a slave to all people to bring many to Christ. When I was with the Jews, I lived like a Jew to bring the Jews to Christ. When I was with those who follow the Jewish law, I too lived under that law. Even though I am not subject to the law, I did

this so I could bring to Christ those who are under the law. When I am with the Gentiles who do not follow the Jewish law, I too live apart from that law so I can bring them to Christ. But I do not ignore the law of God; I obey the law of Christ. When I am with those who are weak, I share their weakness, for I want to bring the weak to Christ. Yes, I try to find common ground with everyone, doing everything I can to save some."

Paul modeled connection in an absolutely beautiful way. Even though he was a man of high stature, a man who had done much for the sake of the Gospel, he loved people, and his single most important focus was leading people to Jesus.

Paul owned a tent-making company that he operated through many of his years in the ministry, in case you didn't know. He worked alongside all sorts of people with various backgrounds and beliefs. He did this to have an open door to share Christ with those who needed his services and products. He was the marketplace minister of his day. He raised many who followed in his footsteps to use their gifts and talents as a way of glorifying God, blessing people, and advancing the Gospel through the people they connected with daily.

I love his words; he didn't cast anyone aside, the Jew, the Gentile (unbelievers of all kinds and beliefs), the weak and broken. He knew exactly how to meet people where they were, just like Jesus did. Paul made it easy for them to connect with him emotionally. He let his passions show through without fear or shame. He would also write, "I am not ashamed of the Gospel of Jesus Christ for it is the POWER of God for salvation." He never shied away from sharing Christ. I'm sure he was strategic in sharing, making connections, building relationships, and waiting for doors of conversation to open. I'm sure he waited for the inevitable questions that would come about his faith to say the right thing at the right time allowing the Holy Spirit to minister to the person's heart.

The New Living Translation for the Scripture verses above uses the phrase "common ground." Paul was able to find common ground with everyone. Connection is about finding common ground so that the person you want to lead to Christ wants to hear what you have to say.

Paul never compromised his faith or God's ways either. He maneuvered magnificently through every twist and turn, keeping his eyes on the prize of winning souls to Jesus. Through it, he allowed people to see his weaknesses and vulnerability, as well as his strengths. People must have thought he was a faith giant! But remember, he wrote, that I may win "some." Not all people were excited to hear his thoughts; however, their rejection never deterred Paul. He kept on moving and shaking and being everything, God had created him to be in his life.

As Paul made connections with the people he encountered, their thoughts began to change. It mattered to them what Paul had to say, his opinions, beliefs, and convictions. He won their hearts and minds for Christ because he met them where they were. He knew how to touch them emotionally, and for that, they hung on his every word.

Paul gave us another critical example of connection in his first letter to the Thessalonians. In Chapter One, Paul wrote about his great affection for the believers. He wrote with such eloquence and love to make sure each person knew that he longed for them and desired that connection with them like a mother longs for and desires her nursing child. He even wrote about how he could have made demands upon them as an apostle, but instead desired a deep-hearted connection with each one.

It's such a beautiful picture of El Shaddai, the multi-breasted one, our God who loves beyond reason and desires nothing more than connection with us. Even as I type these words, I'm flooded with the love of God and our Christ who died so willingly for us so that we could live eternally with Him in a place of perfection through our faith in Jesus Christ. It is, simply, the most beautiful love story ever written.

So, friend, to gain influence, to bring impact, to be successful in life, ministry, and business, we must be willing to connect with the people we want to lead to Christ. Yes, it will require us to be weak with the weak, vulnerable in moments we may not necessarily want to be vulnerable, and open to people we may not initially want to connect with within the moment. I'm telling you right now that those people are heaven sent into your life to bring growth, grace, and influence to you as you respond rightly to them; the way Jesus would respond. Get it? Learning to maneuver those moments with an open heart and unclenched fists will bring a beauty to you that the world will never be able to deny. And, you will look just like Jesus.

Never forget the purpose of influence in the kingdom of God is to advance the Gospel. No matter what you do in life, ministry, and business, all should be done with the single purpose of Jesus Christ being known and received by people. How you connect with people will determine their receptivity to the Gospel and your influence in their life to lead them there.

Remember:

- Make it easy for people to connect with you emotionally.
- Don't be afraid to let your passion show.
- The Apostle Paul was able to connect with people where they were, not compromising, but making that heart connection in a way that they wanted to hear what he had to say.
- He allowed them to see his weakness and vulnerability, as well as his strengths and talents.
- He knew how to touch them emotionally in a compelling way.

- His thoughts and opinions, beliefs, and convictions all mattered to them.

- He always had an eye towards bringing them to Christ and advancing the kingdom of God.

List 3 weaknesses and 3 strengths, then think about how you can connect with others as you become vulnerable in your relationships so that you can influence them for Christ and Kingdom.

1. _____
2. _____
3. _____
4. _____
5. _____
6. _____

Essential No. 7

LOVE

Essential #7 – Love!

I wanted love to be first when I wrote the list of these 7 essentials. However, God ordered it, and He put love last. So interesting to me, but I knew there was a purpose in it that was beyond my comprehension. It's better to follow God, obey His promptings than to do what seems right to us. I know you agree.

The most important thing to remember about love is that everything we do and say, must, must, must, be rooted and grounded in love. When we pray, our prayers should spring from a heart of love. When we listen, remember "auscultate" in the Greek meaning to take a stethoscope and listen to the heart. Even our listening must be rooted in love as we listen to the heart of ourselves and others. Honor is rooted in love, investing too. We never give to get; we give, and we give with a heart of love.

I believe the most significant thing a leader can do is help facilitate the fulfillment of the gifts and callings of others. When leaders are others-minded with a pure heart of love, they will be successful in everything they do. When leaders are more concerned about their advancement than others, it puts them in a place of competing and comparing, and no one ever progresses beyond the place they are in right at that moment. If they do, there's no joy, only striving to achieve something as elusive as bottling sunshine. Leaders who do this hold themselves and others back.

I like that love is number seven because seven is God's number for perfection and completion. It's appropriate. When everything springs from a deep heart of love for others, we will come into wholeness. Shalom, nothing missing, nothing broken, the "sozo" (saved, healed, delivered) life God has for us. It's love that perfects us. The Apostle John wrote about love's perfection. I like to call him the Apostle of Love because he is the disciple whom Jesus loved and the only man left standing at the Cross when Jesus died. He wrote extensively about love and penned in 1 John 4:18, "perfect love casts out all fear." Think about that for a moment. If you are afraid, it means your love is not yet perfected. Holy Spirit is working with you to bring this process to completion; love of God, love of self, love of neighbor. Fear is a spirit, right? Paul wrote, "God has not given us a spirit of fear, but power, love, and a sound mind." Fear is not of God, period. Fear is the polar opposite of faith, hope, belief, and trust. Put fear to flight by reaffirming your faith in God. Fear is defeated when we cast it off us by loving the person who brings fear or doing the things, we fear the most.

Each one of these essentials is part of the character and quality of influential people. I mentioned George Washington earlier. We know of his character, we know that he was a great leader; one of history's most outstanding leaders. His conduct and manner of communication were very intentional, as he treated others with respect and honor. His Rules of Civility were all borne out of love for self and brotherhood. If we lack any of the character qualities I've mentioned in these seven essentials, we probably lack mature love in the areas we struggle in today.

Paul wrote in 1 Corinthians 13:1 that we become "hollow sounds of clanging symbols" if we lack love. Hollow reminds me of a shallow, empty heart. We want to be deep-hearted, authentic, able to connect for their benefit. It's not about us; it's about them. Love started this whole thing in the Garden of Eden. It was all about love, a desire for fellowship and family. So, love started it, and love will finish it.

I've taught Revelation from the perspective of love several times. All through the Book, you can spot the love of God. Often people think of Revelation as a book of war, death, destruction, God is angry, and He's going to make them pay. Therefore, people are afraid (there it is FEAR) of the Book of Revelation. It's actually a beautiful book if you read it from the perspective that God so loved the world that He gave His only begotten son Jesus Christ. When you start seeing through the eyes of love, EVERYTHING changes. And influence begins to grow.

What does love do, how does it look in operation? Love covers faults and disagreements; the Bible says it covers a multitude of sins. It takes no account of suffered wrongs; it's not touchy, fretful, or resentful. Love operates best in challenging situations and relationships; the people we don't want to love are those we need to love. God is entrusting these people to our care. Like submission, we are not challenged to submit until we disagree. Likewise, we have to love when we don't want to love. Love puts others' needs above our own, above the insecurities and impurities that people often experience. Our words and acts must spring from love.

Let God test everything in your life to see IF it is springing from a heart of love. Even the things that feel right. We all know the moments when we fall short. Those are blaring!!! But then there are those things that seem right, sound right, feel right, but in the end, will burn up in the fire. We don't want ANYTHING in our lives to burn up. Why waste your time doing things that will not be blessed in the end. Why am I throwing these thoughts in at this moment? Because, if we truly love, our number one focus should be pleasing God, hearing His words, "Well done faithful one, enter your reward." So remember, whatever doesn't work toward that end must go. Often, these are things where love is not evident. Look at everything. Let God test your motives, thoughts, and actions, adjust where necessary. Die to self so that He can live through you.

When people recognize your selfless love towards them, the doorway of influence opens, and they desire your advice and the wisdom you bring to every situation. You may have to invest a lot of time in your love endeavor; but it will be time that is worth every effort.

It makes me think of my dad! I had so many rough seasons with him. He wasn't a believer, and I desperately wanted him born-again. I'd try to talk with him from time to time; every effort ended in a complete blowup. Finally, after one incident ended horribly, God whispered, "Why don't you just live your life before him?" Hello? Again, a lightbulb moment! Another time, after admitting I had residues of hatred in my heart for my dad, God said, "You MUST love him." I answered, "Then give me YOUR love for Him; I don't know how to love him."

Both encounters with God produced one of the most fantastic love stories between a daughter and her dad. I got to watch God change my father's heart and see him receive Christ right before he went to heaven.

When we love the unlovable, we hold the door open for God to wholly fill and flood that person with His love. And, each time we do what we are created to do in their lives, we gain influence.

Love is powerful and produces insight, awareness, wisdom, and knowledge in our lives. Once we've grown in stature, we can impart into the lives of others. Paul wrote a prayer to the Philippians, communicating his desire that their love would be fully developed and brought to completion. As we cooperate with the plans of God, we grow, causing another awesome thing to happen within us. We approach the day of Christ not stumbling or causing others to stumble. I don't know about you; I desire to finish my race in faith, in full assurance that I have done all God created me to do. More than anything, I want to influence the world with the Gospel of Christ. Developing to the full in love is a key to finishing strong.

When I shared these things with a group of leaders not long ago, I asked them to tell me one way they could love people better than they do right now. I told them they couldn't repeat what someone else said; they had to develop their unique, loving way. I was so blessed by what they shared, each powerful, thought-provoking, and practical enough to be applied in your life today. Here they are;

> Beverly Carter shared, "Love yourself and identify where fear is controlling your love for people. Hatred is not the opposite of love; fear is because fear is the root of all behaviors contrary to Christ."
>
> Rose Flores added, "Put judgment away. You can't love someone and judge them at the same time."
>
> Tracey Schreiber said, "Trample your flesh, apologize, do the opposite of what your flesh wants to do, then you will give Satan a black eye."
>
> Pat Spell Blackwell concluded with, "Research the love language of the person/people you need to demonstrate love to the most. In doing so, you will learn how to fill their love tank and that will change everything."

I'd say these ladies are going to blaze a trail of love across the world that will influence multitudes for Christ! I'm cheering them on all the way.

Now it's your turn, list 5 ways that you can start loving people more today as you demonstrate your love to them in ways that will change their future.

1. _____

2. _____

3. _____

4. _____

5. _____

> "Let love and kindness be the motivation behind all that you do" (1 Cor. 16:14).

Remember,

- Love must be the grounded root of every essential listed above (Ephesians 3:14-21). Without love, our words are reduced to the hollow sounds of clanging cymbals (1 Cor. 13:1, TPT).
- Love is the key to EVERYTHING.
- Love started God's plan, and love will finish His plan (John 3:16).
- Love covers the faults and shortcomings of others (1 Peter 4:8 & Proverbs 10:12). When people

recognize your love for them, they want to hear your advice and the wisdom you bring to every situation.

- When you love without measure, you open the door for God's healing power to flow so that deliverance, healing, repentance, and restoration can come.

- Ask God to give you HIS heart of love for all people and creation. He will!

Final Thoughts

Now that you see the importance of each essential and how developing these character qualities in your life will make you a more influential person, it's time to make an "ALL IN" commitment to building your life, ministry, and business in a way that will open the doorway of opportunity to you, time and time again.

You will gain the favor of both God and man, coupled with a reputation that will precede you in ways you cannot imagine today!

Be consistent moving forward. Success requires consistency in both easy and hard times. You can do it, and as you do, you will leave a legacy for your family, those you minister to throughout your life, and through your business endeavors.

If you want more of what you received here, influential wisdom and imparted strength, connection, mentorship, etc., join me over in the Women of Influence Network at charlanakelly.com/womenofinfluence.

If you desire individualized, focused attention, there's also an opportunity to spend time with me one-on-one. Get all the details at charlanakelly.com/coaching.

Either way! I am for you, cheering as you go. When you succeed, I celebrate!

Much love,

Charlana

Thank Yous & Acknowledgements

First, God, Jesus, Holy Spirit, forever and forever all glory to YOU. Without You, I'm nothing, and with every day I live, I'm aware of this more and more. All gratitude and honor to You!

To my amazing husband Chuck, who is simply the perfect complement to me, we finish each other and support each other in such marvelous ways. Thank you for loving me when, from time to time, I made it hard to do so, and thank you for encouraging me to always get out of my comfort zone. You pushed me hard into television, and even though I wanted to resist, you wouldn't stand for it. Oh, how I love you and thank God for the day you "waltzed" into my life, God's gift! I hope we will dance throughout eternity together.

To my mother, Rose, who taught me about Jesus a long time before I would give my heart entirely to Him, your rewards in heaven must be outstanding! I celebrate you and your sacrificial love. The best cheerleader I could ever have.

To my daddy in heaven, thank you for teaching me Christ-like love even when you did not know Him. You gave me a love for the nations and every human being, one of the greatest gifts I ever received.

To Pat Blackwell and Pastor Leon Wallace, thank you for taking the time to read 7 Essentials to Gain Influence for Success in Life, Ministry, and Business prerelease and giving their thoughts and encouragement to readers regarding the message God birthed in my heart to write.

Thank you to the mentors in my life who had a significant impact on my heart and mind; Lynne Hammond, Billye Brim, Heidi Baker, Francis Frangipane, Carter Conlon, David Wilkerson; I could go on and on. Each of you came into my life at a pivotal moment and your words, divinely inspired, shaped me. God used you mightily, and for that, I am eternally grateful.

To Pastor Tim Gilligan, you taught me for decades, sat with me from time to time, and poured pure wisdom of

God into my heart. You, sir, will never know this side of heaven the impact you have had on my life and family. Tears flood my eyes even now! In a day when biblical literacy is at an all-time low, my mind overflows continually with the true riches of God's Word so profoundly sown into my heart during my time at Meadowbrook Church. I thank God with tears every time I think of you.

Again, to Pastor Leon Wallace, your example of true servant leadership and passion for people have impacted my life in profound ways. Thank you for your inspiring words and opened doorways of freedom to be all God created me to be. Your leadership qualities are those of the giants of faith, and I'm grateful to be in such company. Sir, keep doing what you do; your impact is beyond what you can imagine today.

To Pastors Tim Allen and Larry Bruce, your affirming encouragement and opportunities to stretch my wings and soar to higher heights inspire me in the way I lead others and minister to the masses. You have impacted the trajectory of my life in powerful ways. I am fruit on your tree and for that my heart overflows with a gratitude that is hard to express, nonetheless felt so deeply. May the Lord bless you continually above and beyond anything and everything your heart desires.

To Bishop Dr. Matthew & Angel Meagher, you opened the door to me for television, giving me the opportunity of a lifetime that helped me realize my heart's desire to reach multiple millions (even billions!) of people and nations with the Gospel of Christ. Your friendship and inspired words of encouragement have both soothed my soul and spurred me on to envision more and know that God will fulfill every part of His plan for my life.

To Tim Lowry for opening a broader door into radio, your graciousness and partnership in media have often left me speechless. The future is bright, and I'm excited to see it unfold.

Finally, to all the powerful, influential women who decided to take the journey with me in the Women of Influence Network (Tiffany Renee Blackmon, Pat Blackwell, Beverly Carter, Lori Clifton, Rose Flores, Veronica Harris, Arlene Liner, Kathy Privitera, Lourdes Relyea, Lynn Salinas, Tracey Schreiber, Ashley Shoemake, Tami Vandergriff, Tere Willen, and all those that are to come.) you will impact the world in ways you cannot imagine today. Stay steady, consistent, connected, and faithful to the power Source. He has hold of your life; the days ahead will be astounding.

ABOUT THE AUTHOR

Charlana Kelly is a multiple times author, TV/Radio host, founder of Women of Influence Network, and CEO of SpeakTruth Media Group LLC. She also serves alongside of Pastor Leon Wallace at Good Shepherd Fellowship in a ministerial capacity and is a member of the Houston County Ministerial Association. Her accomplishments are too numerous to note here, suffice is to say, she's ministered around the world, taught in numerous churches, and brought the message of salvation to multiple millions of people. She and her husband of 35 years, Chuck, who is the love of her life, live in historic Crockett Texas where God is doing marvelous things.

You can connect with her at any of these sites:

Website: www.charlanakelly.com

Social Media: @charlanakelly on all platforms

Weekly radio program, Unshakable, listen at:

1043joyfm.com/radio/ every Thursday at 4pm CDT

Podcasts available on all platforms, search "Unshakable with Charlana Kelly"

Weekly TV program, Engage for Influence on Grace TV. Watch live Friday at 7pm CDT or Sunday 7am CDT at www.gracetv.co

On-demand episodes available at: www.youtube.com/c/charlanakellytv

Her books are available at all major online book retailers:

- In Search of the King's Court
- Reaching Out with a Message of Hope
- You Are not Here by Accident
- Irrefutable

- Find & Fuel Your Purpose
- 7 Essentials to Gain Influence for Success in Life, Ministry, and Business
- And coming soon... Engage for Influence

If you are a woman who desires connection, mentorship and support in life, ministry, and business, visit www.charlanakelly.com/womenofinfluence for information about how you can become a member.

If you desire a more individualized focus and want to spend time with Charlana to learn the wisdom and courage it takes to build a strong, vibrant life and ministry for Christ, visit charlanakelly.com/coaching.

www.ingramcontent.com/pod-product-compliance
Lightning Source LLC
Chambersburg PA
CBHW070930080526
44589CB00013B/1460